Play and Discover

ANiMALS

Caryn Jenner

W
FRANKLIN WATTS
LONDON·SYDNEY

First published in 2014
by Franklin Watts

Copyright © Franklin Watts 2014

Franklin Watts
338 Euston Road
London NW1 3BH

Franklin Watts Australia
Level 17/207 Kent Street
Sydney, NSW 2000

Series editor: Sarah Peutrill
Design: Basement68

Dewey number: 590
HB ISBN: 978 1 4451 3135 1
Library ebook ISBN: 978 1 4451 3136 8

Printed in China

Franklin Watts is a division
of Hachette Children's Books,
an Hachette UK company.

www.hachette.co.uk

Picture credits: adipelcz/istockphoto: front cover main. Africa Studio/Shutterstock: 15bl. Balazs Justin/Shutterstock: 10t, 23cbc. Hung Chung Chih/Shutterstock: 5tl. Civdis/Shutterstock: 14t, 23br. Copit/Shutterstock: 5br. creative/Shutterstock: 4c. dtriff/Shutterstock: 15t, 23cbcl. Sebastian Duda/Shutterstock: 4b. Nanette Grebe/Shutterstock: 11r. hfng/Shutterstock: 5tr. Olga_i/Shutterstock: 10b, 22bl, 22cr, 23cr. irin-k/Shutterstock: 16t, 23cbl. igor kisselev/Shutterstock: 19cr. Brian Lasenby/Shutterstock: 12-13, 23bcl. Tom Linster/Shutterstock: 18l, 18br, 23cl, 23tc. mast3r/Shutterstock:9b. Svetlana Mihailova/Shutterstock: 19l. Neirfy/Shutterstock: 2b, 7. Czintos Odon/Shutterstock: 16br, 23bl. paffy/Shutterstock: 17. panda3800/Shutterstock: 5bl. Patrick Foto/Shutterstock: 13t. Pefkos/Shutterstock: 9bg. Thomas Perkins/Dreamstime: 14b. Graur Razvan/Shutterstock: 1, 6, 23tr. Tom Reichner/Shutterstock: 11bl, 22tc, 22br, 23cbr. samzsolti/Shutterstock: 12tr. 23c. Victoria Savostianova/Shutterstock: front cover tr. sevenke/Shutterstock: 21b. Claudia Steininger/Shutterstock: 2t, 8, 22c, 22tr, 23cl. A. Storm Photography/Shutterstock: 21b. Kuttelvaserova Stuchelova/Shutterstock: 21b. Tomartika/Dreamstime: 21l. Tsekhmister/Shutterstock: 3b, 19br. alex virid/Shutterstock: 16bl, 23bc. wizdata/Shutterstock: 20, 23tcl. Every attempt has been made to clear copyright. Should there be any inadvertent omission please apply to the publisher for rectification.

Contents

All sorts of animals

There are lots of different animals in the world.

Some animals are big and some are little.

Some animals are furry and some are feathery.

Some animals are scaly and some are slimy.

Which animal do you like?

Ears

My cat has two big ears.

She can hear a mouse squeak.

6

I made a cat mask.
It had big ears too.

Paws

My dog walks
on four paws.

Moving

A monkey climbs.

A horse gallops.

10

A rabbit hops.

Look at me! I can hop too.

Hiding

This frog is green like the grass. Can you see it?

Look very carefully. Can you find the stick insect?

I'm hiding. Can you see me?

How could I hide better?

13

Patterns

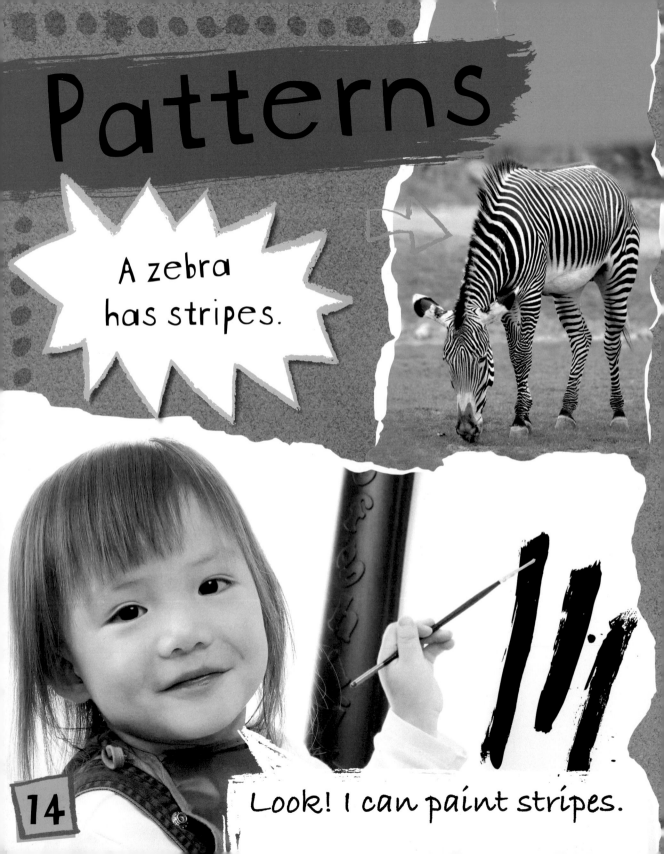

A zebra has stripes.

Look! I can paint stripes.

14

Minibeasts

Look! I see a ladybird.

Here are a wiggly worm and a slimy snail.

I see lots of minibeasts with my magnifying glass.

17

Changing

When this caterpillar grows up, what will it be?

It will be a butterfly, like this one!

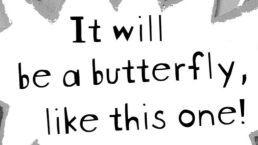

I'm using modelling clay to make a caterpillar and a butterfly.

Homes

These birds live in a cosy nest.

It is made from grass, leaves and moss.

I'm using paper to make a cosy nest for these toy birds.

With your friends

Mix and match animals

Play this fun game with your friends. Stick pictures of animals onto card, then cut the animal pictures in half. Give each player one half of an animal picture. Players sit in a circle and hold up their pictures. The aim is to look around the circle and find the other half of your animal. For example, the back end of a dog will be a match for the front end of the dog. Or you and your friends can try making mixed-up animals, such as putting the front end of a cat with the back end of an elephant! How silly is that?

Bird

Butterfly

Cat

Caterpillar

Dog

Frog

Horse

Ladybird

Leopard

Monkey

Rabbit

Snail

Stick insect

Worm

Zebra

Index

Notes for parents and teachers

Paws – Dip the children's hands and feet in paint and press onto paper or card to make handprints and footprints. Discuss the fact that dogs and other animals have four paws, while humans have two hands and two feet. Show pictures of other animal paw prints and compare them to the dog's paw prints.

Ears – Draw a simple outline of a cat's face (or other animal) on card and cut it out. Cut out eyeholes and attach a piece of elastic or string. The children can wear their masks to role play being cats, purring and miaowing. They can pretend to be sleepy cats curled up in a ball, or lively cats chasing a squeaky mouse.

Moving – Children can practise a range of physical skills by copying the movements of different animals. Ask them to climb like a monkey, gallop like a horse, hop like a rabbit and copy the movements of other animals too. Can they pretend to fly like a bird or swim like a fish?

Hiding – Play a game of hide and seek with the children. Encourage the 'hiders' to be still and silent and try to blend into the environment so they won't be found, and encourage the 'seekers' to use their senses of sight and hearing to find their friends.

Patterns – Painting zebra stripes and leopard spots encourages children to look closely and copy markings, helping with handwriting skills. Ask the children if they can think of other animals that have special patterns, such as tigers or giraffes, and see if they can copy those markings too.

Minibeasts – Take the children to a garden or park to observe minibeasts up close through a magnifying glass. Watching minibeasts in their natural habitat helps children to understand that there are lots of different creatures all around us, even if they aren't easily seen.

Changing – Read *The Very Hungry Caterpillar*, by Eric Carle and discuss how caterpillars turn into butterflies. Have the children use modelling clay to make a caterpillar and a butterfly. Ask them to point out the differences between the two, eg, a caterpillar crawls while a butterfly flies.

Homes – Have the children fill a box with shredded paper or straw to make a pretend birds' nest. Discuss how birds' nests are usually in high up places because birds fly. Show pictures of other animal homes and discuss why different animals live in different sorts of homes.